CLASSIC CARS

VHK 282M

Introduction

What, exactly, makes a car a classic? When prices paid by collectors started rising in the early 1980s, the definition generally applied to interesting cars made between 1945 and 1970. British laws still reflect this: any car made before 1 January 1973 can be driven without the owner needing to pay Vehicle Excise Duty, because it's deemed 'historic'. Before then, motoring enthusiasts had decided unofficial categories. 'Veteran' cars were those built from 1885 to 1903; 'Edwardian' cars from 1904 to 1914; 'Vintage' cars from 1919 to 1930; and any worthwhile car built from 1931 to 1939 was declared a 'Post-Vintage Thoroughbred'.

However, as new generations of enthusiasts began to appreciate cars made since 1970, the old divisions became less relevant. And nostalgia mattered just as much as historical significance.

We've discarded all the old arguments and prejudices so the I-Spy Book Of Classic Cars can span the history of motoring, from the 10.5bhp (brake horse power) of the Austin Seven to the 1001 bhp of the Bugatti Veyron. The one thing every car in this book has in common, though, is a 'fan base' – a significant number of enthusiasts (often formed into an owners' club) who admire, enjoy, preserve and promote their chosen makes and models of car.

So Bond Bug owners are just as passionate as those lucky enough to possess a Bentley... and a Smart is just as important in car 'evolution' as an Austin Seven.

Spying any of the cars in this book on British roads is unusual. None are common sights in everyday traffic, although most have distinctive features that we've highlighted. Each one, however, is regularly enjoyed by its proud owner.

How to use your I-SPY book

We've selected these cars to reflect the range of classics you're likely to spy in Britain. They're arranged in date order so you can see how cars of each era compare. Earlier ones are easier to spy during summertime – owners prefer driving them in fine weather. However, you could boost your score at a car show, motoring festival, rally, or a museum like the National Motor Museum in Hampshire, the British Road Transport Museum in Coventry, or the Cars Of The Stars Museum in Cumbria.

You need 1000 points to send off for your I-Spy certificate (see page 64) but there are masses of points in every book. As you make each I-Spy, write your score in the box.

I-SPY TITLES AVAILABLE:

- Ancient Britain
- Birds
- Cars
- Classic Cars
- Creepy Crawlies
- Flags
- Nature
- On a Car Journey
- On a Train Journey
- Trees
- Wild Flowers
- Working Vehicles

DE DION-BOUTON
1900-1913

This two-seater is seen in large numbers on the annual London-Brighton veteran car run. Practical and popular when new, it was always equipped with a single-cylinder engine, a power unit so compact that the engine bay looks half-empty.

I-SPY points: 40

Date:_____

ROLLS-ROYCE 40/50HP
1906-1925

The 40/50 was better known as the Ghost or Silver Ghost. The engine is a refined 7-litre straight-six...but the car had no front-wheel brakes until 1924! Every Ghost looks different because customers could specify any kind of bodywork they liked.

I-SPY points: 45

Date:_____

3

FORD MODEL T
1908-1927

More than 15 million Model Ts
found buyers – a sales record
unbroken until 1972. The secret
of its success was its ruggedness,
reliability, and high ground
clearance to deal with rough
American roads. Model Ts were
also built in Britain from 1911.

I-SPY points: 30

Date: _____

VAUXHALL
PRINCE HENRY
1911-1914

This big four-seater tourer
was also a sports car. It
gained its name from an
aristocrat who sponsored
the 1910 Prince Henry
Trial in Germany, a 1200-
mile event in which the big
Vauxhall did surprisingly
well. The original engine was a
fast-revving 3-litre, later uprated
to 4-litre.

I-SPY points: 45

Date: _____

I-SPY points: 40

Date: _____ ◯

MORRIS COWLEY
1015-1926

This Morris gained its 'Bull-nose' nickname because the domed top of its radiator shell looked like a 0.303 bullet. The Cowley was a cheaper version of the Morris Oxford, and features a 26bhp, 1.5-litre engine and artillery-type wheels. It was one of Britain's first really successful models.

CITROËN TYPE C
1922-1926

This little Citroen proved easy for just about anyone to drive and maintain, and performance was adequate with an 11bhp engine. Early Cs were usually painted a distinctive yellow, and so were often dubbed 'Citron' – the French for lemon! Some 81,000 were sold.

I-SPY points: 45 ◯

Date: _____

AUSTIN SEVEN
1922-1939

Sir Herbert Austin's first 'real car in miniature' was hurried into production in 1923, but quickly became a motoring legend. It is very light and, although there's just room for four people, the tiny 747cc, 10.5bhp engine struggles to pull a fully-loaded Seven along.

I-SPY points: 25

Date: _____

BENTLEY 3-LITRE
1921-1929

The rough roads and race circuits of the 1920s meant sports cars had to be big and tough, and Bentley proved the point in the Le Mans 24-hour endurance race. Two of Bentley's victories there, in 1924 and 1927, were taken by the sturdy 3-litre cars.

I-SPY points: 40

Date: _____

ROLLS-ROYCE
20/25 *1929-1936*

Although a small car by
Rolls-Royce standards, the
20/25 model still offered
a 3.7-litre, six-cylinder
engine. Just like all pre-
1939 Rolls-Royce cars, the
20/25 was supplied as a
rolling chassis only – you
commissioned your own
body from your chosen
'coachbuilder'; many elegant-
looking cars resulted.

I-SPY points: 30

Date: _____

MORRIS MINOR
1929-1934

An open-top version of the
Minor, with a canvas roof made
headlines for being the first
British car offered for sale at just
£100 – ensuring it became one of
the most popular cars around. It's
a little larger than the rival Austin
Seven, better equipped with an
847cc engine, and, with a 55mph
top speed, faster too.

I-SPY points: 40

Date: _____

I-SPY points: 30

Date: _____

AUSTIN 10 *1932-1947*

A 1.1-litre sidevalve engine gives this well-liked family car a top speed of about 55mph. It proved popular in suburban Britain, and the styling was updated in 1934 and 1937 to keep customers loyal. The range of bodywork options includes versions named after British towns like Cambridge, Sherborne and Ripley.

FORD MODEL Y 8HP *1932-1937*

This trusty little car, often called the Ford Popular, was built exclusively in Europe, but was actually designed in the USA. There was a choice of two- or four-door options, with the cheapest two-door model the only solid bodied saloon car ever sold in Britain for £100. The 933cc, 23bhp engine well suited the need for economical motoring.

I-SPY points: 30

Date: _____

CITROËN TRACTION AVANT *1934-1957*

Traction Avant is French for front-wheel drive – just one of the many features of this innovative and stylish car. Launched as the 1.3-litre Citroën 7A in 1934, this was the first European mass produced car. Later models, while sharing a similar shape, offered bigger engines and better interior space.

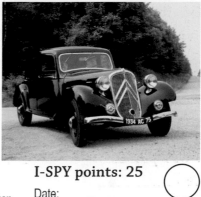

I-SPY points: 25

Date: _____

MG TA MIDGET *1936-1939*

This small sports car set the pattern for MG's two-seaters for almost two decades, with separate mudguards, a 'slab' fuel tank across the back and the spare wheel fixed to the tail. The handling and ride are good, and the 52bhp 1.3-litre engine gives the TA a top speed of 80mph. Over 3000 were sold.

I-SPY points: 30

Date: _____

9

LANCIA APRILIA
1937-1949
Compared to other family cars of the era, the Aprilia certainly looks streamlined. As, indeed, it is: it was one of the first production cars to be aerodynamically shaped using wind tunnel testing. No wonder it can hit 80mph. It has all-round independent suspension and Lancia's characteristic V4 engine.

I-SPY points: 35

Date:

SS 100 JAGUAR
1935-1939
One of the coolest cars of the late 1930s, for many the SS 100 represented the perfect sports car. Some were used to win rallies. The 3.5-litre model, introduced in 1938, can break the 100mph barrier. SS later adopted this model's name to become Jaguar Cars.

I-SPY points: 30

Date:

WILLYS JEEP MB
1942-1945

Purpose-designed for the US Army, the 'General Purpose' (or GP, which morphed into 'Jeep') was the first lightweight vehicle with four-wheel drive. It has a no-frills appearance because it was meant for battlefields; only later did farmers and sportsmen learn to admire its off-road ability.

I-SPY points: 30

Date:

VOLKSWAGEN
BEETLE *1938-2003*

The curvy outline of the Beetle became world-famous because, wherever it was sold, people found its build quality and reliability outstanding. It appeared in the late 1930s as a German 'people's car'; the last of over 21 million examples was made in Mexico in 2003. Over that time, its rear-mounted, air-cooled engines ranged from 1.1- to 1.6-litre.

I-SPY points: 10

Date:

BRISTOL 400
1947-1950

The Bristol Aeroplane Company started car manufacture with this high–performance saloon – later it probably would have been called a GT (for Gran Turismo) car. Its responsive 2-litre engine was derived from the pre-war BMW 328's. Its smooth, wind-cheating body helps the 400 exceed 90mph.

I-SPY points: 35

Date: _____

CITROËN 2CV
1948-1990

You only need to look at the 2CV to see how its nickname of 'tin snail' arose! This go-anywhere utility car was designed to carry French countryfolk, and their cargoes of eggs, across rutted fields in economical comfort. So the 'powerpack' of air-cooled engine and front-wheel drive are thrifty on petrol, while long-travel suspension ensures a soft ride.

I-SPY points: 5

Date: _____

JAGUAR XK120
1948-1954

Sensational when introduced, and a beautiful looking car even today, this two-seater really put Jaguar on the world map as a great marque. The view along the long bonnet was just as exciting: a brand new twin camshaft, straight-six engine with a lively 160bhp of power. The 120mph top speed of early models was almost unheard-of at the time.

I-SPY points: 30

Date: _____

LAND ROVER SERIES 1 *1948-1958*

This is the first Land Rover. It took the best of the war-time Jeep and improved it as a useful vehicle for farmers. Therefore, it featured four-wheel drive, but also boxy aluminium bodywork and a choice of lengths. Rover underestimated demand for these workhorses; soon Land Rovers were outselling Rover cars.

I-SPY points: 35

Date: _____

MORRIS MINOR
1948-1971

The attractively-curved Minor became one of Britain's best-loved cars…and also the first to exceed the one million sales mark. At first, its 918cc motor meant it was underpowered (later fixed with new engines), but excellent suspension and steering made it delightful to drive. Look out for Minors as a saloon, convertible, van, pick-up, and the distinctive, wood-framed Traveller estate.

I-SPY points: 10

Date:

JOWETT JAVELIN
1949-1954

This was a surprising car from Yorkshire-based Jowett. It was an advanced design with a new four-cylinder engine mounted flat on its side, modern aerodynamic styling, a roomy cabin, and good roadholding. Its 1.5-litre engine propelled it to 80mph. It sold quite well and many survive today.

I-SPY points: 35

Date:

TRIUMPH RENOWN *1949-1954*

The Standard Motor Company took control of Triumph in 1954, and launched the Triumph 1800 saloon six years later. The 2.1-litre Triumph Renown is an evolution of this elegant car. They share 'razor-edge' styling intended to evoke the crisp lines of an expensive limousine like a Rolls-Royce. Room and visibility are also advantages of this body design.

I-SPY points: 35

Date: _____

MG TD *1949-1953*

It's quite unusual to see an MG TD on British roads; not because they have all been carted off to the scrapyard, but because the vast majority of the 30,000 TDs made were exported to the USA. It still looks like a 1930s roadster, but it has 1950-standard steering and front suspension, and well over 80mph is possible with the impressive 61bhp engine in the MkII version.

I-SPY points: 35

Date:

15

PORSCHE 356
1950-1965

Porsche owes its supercar image today to the little 356. Ferdinand Porsche created it as his idea of the perfect weekend sports car, and based it on the rear-engined, air-cooled Volkswagen Beetle he'd designed in the 1930s. However, the 356 soon

evolved away from the humble VW, eventually coming in four body styles and with engines offering up to 90bhp.

I-SPY points: 35

Date: _____

FORD CONSUL
MK I *1951-1956*

The 1.5-litre Consul was a turning point for Ford: it was the company's first car with a unitary-construction body. It was the first Ford with an overhead-valve engine and also the world's first car with 'MacPherson strut'

independent front suspension; these features combined to make the 75mph Consul feel very modern to drive.

I-SPY points: 30

Date: _____

BENTLEY R-TYPE CONTINENTAL
1952-1955

This was the fastest four-seater on sale in 1952, capable of 124mph. The modified Bentley R-type was clothed in fastback, light aluminium bodywork, wind tunnel-tested by Bentley but handmade by London coachbuilder HJ Mulliner. Almost all of the 207 cars built survive, so you may be lucky enough to spy one.

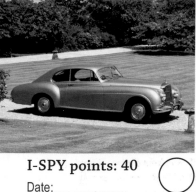

I-SPY points: 40

Date: _____

TRIUMPH TR2
1953-1955

The TR2 is a basic sports car but also a powerful one. Its 2.1-litre four-cylinder engine produces 90bhp, which means it could zoom up to 108mph. Before the age of five-speed gearboxes, a fourth gear overdrive option helped to make it relaxing on long trips but, to keep costs down, flimsy side screens acted as door windows.

I-SPY points: 30

Date: _____

BMW ISETTA
1955-1963

Clever thinking by Italian fridge maker Isotherm produced this 'cabin scooter'...or bubble car, as most people called it. BMW built its own version and, amazingly, it was very popular. With a little air-cooled engine in the back, the whole front of the car swings open as one large door. As a four-wheeler (there was a three-wheeler, too), the rear wheels are just 20 inches apart.

I-SPY points: 35

Date: _____

CITROËN DS
1955-1975

The shark-like DS profile remains unique but, apart from everything you can see – like the single-spoke steering wheel and the rear indicators mounted in the roof – the front-wheel drive saloon came jam-packed with innovation. The hydropneumatic suspension is self-levelling, while gear change, clutch and brakes are all power-assisted.

I-SPY points: 20

Date: _____

18

VOLKSWAGEN KARMANN-GHIA
1955-1974

This sporty 2+2-seater car, offered as a coupé and a convertible, has striking lines from the Italian design house of Ghia, although the bodies were built in the high-quality workshops of Germany's Karmann coachbuilding company. Yet, under those fine clothes, the car is pure VW Beetle!

I-SPY points: 25

Date: _____

RENAULT DAUPHINE
1956-1967

Like Volkswagen, Renault once favoured rear-mounted engines. This neat little saloon was popular across Europe, with over 2m sold. In Britain, Dauphines were used as the country's first minicabs, despite not being very roomy inside. With an 845cc engine, performance is modest, at 70mph flat-out.

I-SPY points: 35

Date: _____

FIAT 500 *1957-1977*

The cute looks of this tiny economy car – introduced as the Nuova 500, to replace an older model – are so adored that the latest Fiat 500 has revived the same, egg-like shape. The one shown here was cramped, noisy and slow, with an air–cooled, twin-cylinder engine at the back, but it was still hugely popular.

I-SPY points: 20

Date: _____

AUSTIN FX4 TAXI
1958-1997

You still see plenty of FX4-type cabs plying for business around London, the city synonymous with this hard-working classic. It has room for five in the back but just the driver upfront. Many engines were fitted over the years, most of them rather raucous diesels and almost all are black.

I-SPY points: 10

Date: _____

AUSTIN-HEALEY SPRITE MK I
1958-1961

With cheeky headlights sitting on the bonnet top, no wonder fans of this tiny sports car named it the "Frogeye". The whole front part of the body lifts to reveal the 848cc engine, but at the back, there's no boot lid – you have to cram your luggage in from behind the two seats!

I-SPY points: 25

Date: _____

VAUXHALL CRESTA PA *1958-1962*

This large family saloon set the trend in the late 1950s, with its prominent rear fins, elaborate chrome trim and wraparound windscreen heavily influenced by contemporary American cars. Under the bonnet, an unstressed six-cylinder engine was more than adequate to cope with Britain's then-new motorways.

I-SPY points: 25

Date: _____

AUSTIN-HEALEY
3000 *1959-1967*

Collectors love this stylish, low-slung, high-powered sports car with its growling 2.9-litre engine, and a snug cockpit from which to hang out the elbow while roaring around country lanes; many of the 41,000 cars built are cherished. It can do 120mph despite a bone-shaking ride.

I-SPY points: 30

Date:_____

FORD ANGLIA
105E *1959-1967*

Since JK Rowling first featured the Anglia in her *Harry Potter* books, the little saloon has become familiar to a whole new generation. Our grandparents knew it as one of Britain's most popular small cars in the early 1960s, with a particularly responsive engine and, thanks to the oddly-shaped rear window, genuine character.

I-SPY points: 20

Date:_____

22

JAGUAR MK II
1959-1967

Jaguar's series of compact sports saloons began with the 2.4-litre in 1955, but the Mk II cars – with 2.4-, 3.4- and 3.8-litre straight-six engines – were vastly improved in drivability, style and practicality. The 3.8 is capable on both road and race track, with 220bhp on tap and 126mph possible.

I-SPY points: 20

Date: _____

TRIUMPH HERALD
1959-1971

This two–door, four-seater is unusual for its separate chassis, all-independent suspension, and trendy shape. The first version had a 948cc engine driving the rear wheels, but from the mid-1960s the Herald 1200 had an 1147cc, 43bhp unit, giving a 75mph top speed.

I-SPY points: 15

Date: _____

AMPHICAR
1961-1963

Fifty years after it was launched, the Amphicar remains the most successful attempt yet to sell an amphibious car to the motoring public. It can do 70mph on tarmac and 7mph on rivers, and the steering wheel can control either front wheels or rudders! One Amphicar crossed the English Channel.

I-SPY points: 40

Date: _____

JAGUAR E-TYPE
1961-1975

Still regarded as one of the most beautiful sports cars of all time, the original E-type boasted Jaguar's potent 3.8-litre engine. Buyers were amazed that it cost half the price of an Aston Martin DB4 and yet, at 145mph, was 5mph faster. The last cars, the Series III, pack an incredible V12 engine; they're easily identifiable by softer contours and a larger, flatter frontal air.

I-SPY points: 25

Date: _____

JAGUAR MK X
1961-1966

Although the E-type was hot news in 1961, many buyers yearned to own Jaguar's other new model: the Mk X. It was the longest and widest car Britain produced but, despite its bulk, it went like the wind. The sleek styling and opulent passenger compartment made it hugely desirable among celebrities.

I-SPY points: 30

Date: _____

MG MIDGET
1961-1979

An old MG name was revived for this fun two-seater sports cars (an almost identical Austin-Healey Sprite edition was also available). Engines ranged from 948cc in the Mk I to 1275cc in the Mk IV and then, from 1975, the Midget 1500 took over, with both a bigger engine and black rubber bumpers to single it out.

I-SPY points: 10

Date: _____

MINI COOPER
1961-1971

In 1959, the cleverly packaged Mini redefined small cars – the engine was mounted across the front, turning the front wheels, with its gearbox tucked underneath, allowing maximum cabin space. In highly-tuned twin fuel tank Cooper form, it became a rapid road car, and unbeatable in rallying; visual differences from lesser Minis include a contrasting-colour roof, and perforated wheels.

I-SPY points: 15

Date: _____

VOLVO P1800
1961-1972

Volvo's two-seater P1800 won many admirers, particularly after it became a regular sight on TV in the adventure series *The Saint*. At first it was built in Britain but in 1963 switched to Sweden, at which point it became the P1800S and gained an engine size increase from 1.8 to 2.0 litres. The robust P1800S can achieve 115mph.

I-SPY points: 25

Date: _____

26

AC/SHELBY COBRA *1962-1968*

Created in California by Texan racing driver Carroll Shelby, the gorgeous Cobra is a hybrid: Britain's AC body/chassis powered by America's Ford V8 engine. This combination of light weight and plentiful horsepower produces lightning acceleration – enough to have regularly beaten Ferraris on the race track.

I-SPY points: 40

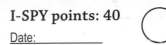

Date: _____

LOTUS ELAN
1962-1973

What you can see on the Elan is the very pretty two-seater bodywork, the pop-up headlights and, on the later Elan Sprint, some groovy two-tone paintjobs. What you can't see is the backbone chassis beneath which, with all-independent suspension and Lotus's wonderful twin-cam engine, make the Elan a fine-handling machine.

I-SPY points: 30

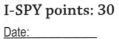

Date: _____

27

HILLMAN IMP
1963-1976

There was much to recommend this boxy but imaginative little car – its terrific, aluminium 875cc engine; its rear window opening as a luggage hatch – but it suffered some teething problems...and fierce competition from the Mini. Over 440 000 were sold, and it's one of the few cars to have been built in Scotland.

I-SPY points: 25

Date: _____

PORSCHE 911
1963-1997

The last air-cooled Porsche 911 was made in 1997, but it wasn't so very different from the first cars of 34 years earlier. They all share a rear-mounted, flat-six-cylinder engine, excellent performance – the Turbo models in particular – and the iconic 911 shape; even a totally new body in 1989 looked little different from previous 911s.

I-SPY points: 10

Date: _____

28

ROVER P6 *1963-1976*

To 21st century eyes, this seems like any typical 1960s car, but the initial 2000 model was one of the first 'executive' saloons – sporty to drive, luxurious, and with four-wheel disc brakes. The later 3500 version has a V8 engine; a badge on the radiator grille identifies it.

I-SPY points: 15

Date:_____

ASTON MARTIN DB5 *1963-1965*

You would have needed to be a successful individual to have afforded a DB5...a bit like *secret agent 007* who, as portrayed by actor Sean Connery, drove one in the classic *James Bond* film *Goldfinger*. A handsome and handmade, 150mph car, they're worth a fortune today – especially the very rare convertible.

I-SPY points: 30

Date:_____

FORD MUSTANG I
1964-1973

Each year, the styling of the original series Mustang evolved, but these two-door, four-seater cars remained hugely popular as sporty cruisers in suburban America. A few found their way to Britain, including some of the very cool convertibles. Most had a six-cylinder engine but powerful V8s were also offered.

I-SPY points: 30

Date: _____

LANCIA FULVIA COUPÉ *1965-1976*

The Lancia Fulvia was a square-shaped saloon that was never popular in Britain. But the beautiful Coupé edition was always desirable; Fiat took Lancia over in 1969, and fans consider the Fulvia the last 'real' Lancia. The 1.3- or 1.6-litre engines drove the front wheels; the fastest editions could manage 115mph.

I-SPY points: 35

Date: _____

MGB GT *1965-1979*

The MGB comes in two forms, as a two-seater open top roadster and this attractive two-seater GT coupé featuring a tailgate rear door. The power unit was always a 1.8-litre four-cylinder engine, although 2600 examples were built with a 3.5-litre V8, turning it into a 125mph car. If you see one with bulky, black rubber bumpers then it's a post-1974 example.

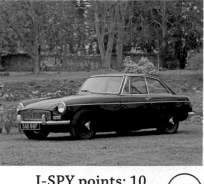

I-SPY points: 10

Date: _____

RENAULT 16
1965-1979

The 1.5- or 1.6-litre 16 was the world's first large family car with a hatchback tailgate and rear seats that fold to increase luggage space. Look inside and you'll see the gearlever is mounted on the steering column, instead of on the floor, to increase front legroom.

I-SPY points: 10

Date: _____

ROLLS-ROYCE SILVER SHADOW

1965-1979

The man responsible for the simple, elegant lines of the Silver Shadow once described it as a "flying drawing room", such was the level of luxury on the inside with rich leather upholstery and gleaming walnut trim. The upright radiator grille, 'flying lady' mascot and four round headlamps lend a stately air.

I-SPY points: 15

Date: _____

SAAB 96 *1960-1979*

Here in its element as a surprisingly successful international rally car, Saab's eager 96 had an air-cooled, three-cylinder engine of only 841cc (later, a 1.5-litre Ford V4 replaced it) driving the front wheels. Its aerodynamic shape betrayed Saab's origins in aircraft manufacture.

I-SPY points: 25

Date: _____

JENSEN INTERCEPTOR
1966-1976

Here's one of the most desirable cars of the 1960s. The Interceptor was British-made but used a US-made Chrysler V8 engine, while the styling, complete with a large, curved glass tailgate, came from Italy. The outwardly similar Jensen FF pioneered the use of four-wheel drive and anti-lock brakes on production cars, revolutionary at the time.

I-SPY points: 25

Date: _____

LOTUS EUROPA
1966-1975

Britain beat even the mighty Lamborghini in the race to offer a mid-engined road car – a layout that had revolutionised racing car design – to the public. Amazing roadholding the Europa certainly has, but rear visibility is a problem with that flattened van styling, and the driver and passenger almost lie down in their seats.

I-SPY points: 30

Date: _____

ALFA ROMEO
SPIDER *1966-1993*

First seen as the pretty Duetto with a neat, tapering tail treatment, Alfa's Spider was destined for long-term popularity as it was delightful to drive with any of the engine sizes available from 1.3 to 2.0-litre. However, the Spider was comprehensively updated several times with new rear-end styling.

I-SPY points: 15
Date: _____

MERCEDES-BENZ
280SL *1967-1971*

The elegant shape of this two-seater roadster was first seen in 1963 as the 230SL, but four years later the engine was upgraded from a 2.3- to a 2.8-litre unit, which gave the car near-120mph capability. Every car came with its own detachable hardtop, to make it enjoyable all year round.

I-SPY points: 30
Date: _____

NSU RO80 *1967-1977*

The RO80 has an engine with twin rotors instead of conventional pistons to convert pressure into power. Called a Wankel engine after engineer Dr Felix Wankel, it makes the car smooth, quiet and fast – it easily manage 110mph. This engine sometimes proved unreliable and thirsty, but the RO80 was always admired for its handsome, timeless styling.

I-SPY points: 30

Date: _____

FERRARI 365 GTB/4 *1968-1974*

Under that long, long bonnet lives a superb, 4.4-litre V12 engine to rocket this gold-plated classic to over 170mph. This was one of the world's ultimate cars of the early 1970s, and usually referred to by its unofficial nickname of 'Daytona'. Yet quite a large number were sold, 1426 in total, so you may be lucky enough to see one scream past.

I-SPY points: 40

Date: _____

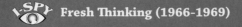
MORGAN PLUS 8

1968-2004

It's hard to tell the age of a Plus 8 because, outwardly, there was little change to the car over its amazing 36 years on sale. Plus, Morgan styling has barely altered since the 1930s. Setting the Plus 8 apart from other Morgans is its use of a powerful V8 engine, as found in Range Rovers. Up to 125mph is possible...but hold on to your hat!

I-SPY points: 30

Date: _____

VOLKSWAGEN TRANSPORTER KOMBI *1968-today*

From carrying surfboards down to the beach in California to chugging across a baking hot Australia, Volkswagen's long-serving, rear-engined van became a trusted friend for active people. The air-cooled engines range from 1.6- to 2.0-litre, and this 'box on wheels' was frequently converted into a mobile home.

I-SPY points: 10

Date: _____

AUSTIN MAXI
1969-1981

The Maxi was the first British car with a fifth door, or hatchback, and folding rear seats, which turned it into a very useful vehicle for occasional cargo-carrying and for going on driving holidays. Available in 1.5- and 1.7-litre forms, it was unusual at the time for having a five-speed gearbox.

I-SPY points: 25

Date: _____

I-SPY points: 35

Date: _____

'FERRARI' DINO
246 GT *1969-1973*

Although made and sold by Ferrari, you'll search in vain for the black-on-yellow 'prancing horse' logo usually seen on cars from this Italian carmaker. It was known, officially, as just the Dino. This 150mph sports car is mid-engined, its 2.4-litre V6 positioned behind the cockpit. There's also a rare Spider model, with a lift-out roof panel.

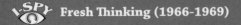

FORD CAPRI MK1
1969-1974

Like America's Mustang, the Capri mixed sleek sports car looks with family saloon reliability. Ford aimed to allow buyers to create their own cars, so there were several trim packages and seven engine options, the most potent being a 3.0-litre V6 making the Capri a 120mph car. The air intakes behind the doors look good...but they're fakes!

I-SPY points: 25

Date: _____

RELIANT SCIMITAR GTE
1969-1990

No-one had thought of combining the practicality of an estate car with the acceleration and style of a sports coupé before the Scimitar. A glass tailgate at the back opens on to a luggage area that can be made huge with the rear seats folded. The bodywork is plastic, and the 3.0-litre engine comes from Ford. An enlarged, but similar, Scimitar was launched in 1976.

I-SPY points: 15

Date: _____

BOND BUG
1970-1974

One of the most extraordinary cars ever to hit British roads, the Bug was a cheap-to-run fun car for young drivers; its 'tricycle' status meant it could be driven on a motorbike license. Instead of individual doors, the whole upper section of the car lifts up as one giant canopy. The triangular, plastic body was offered in just one colour: bright orange!

I-SPY points: 35

Date: _____

DATSUN 240Z
1970-1973

Japan had a reputation for making copies of Western cars until this sporty Datsun came along and proved the country could make a fast and stylish GT. The 2.4-litre straight six-cylinder and all-round independent suspension were rugged enough to make the 125mph 240Z an accomplished rally car too. Datsun became Nissan in 1985.

I-SPY points: 35

Date: _____

FORD CORTINA MK III *1970-1976*

Ford's Cortina, in four different series, dominated the British best-seller list for 20 years. The wide range of family saloons and estates offered great value and mechanical simplicity. The Mk III introduced rack-and-pinion steering and comfortable coil-spring suspension; its wavy side styling was often compared to the curves of a Coca-Cola bottle.

I-SPY points: 20

Date: _____

RANGE ROVER
1970-1996

Britain really led the world in 1970 with the launch of the first Range Rover. It bridged the gap between the four-wheel drive Land Rover and the luxurious Rover saloon, and kick-started the trend for people to use 4x4 vehicles as everyday cars. At first only available as a two-door with a four-door option added in 1980, most have a gutsy V8 engine.

I-SPY points: 10

Date: _____

TRIUMPH STAG
1970-1976

This glamorous convertible has a T-shaped roll-over bar linking the windscreen with the rest of the body, to offer protection if the car turns over in a crash. It's a full four-seater, with plenty of power from its 3.0-litre V8 engine. Some Stags have a detachable hardtop.

I-SPY points: 15

Date:

LAMBORGHINI COUNTACH
1971-1990

The Countach has been turning heads since it first appeared. The striking, wedge-shaped lines were the work of Italian specialist Bertone, and there is a V12 engine mounted in the middle of the chassis. The car's doors open upwards, mimicking a scissors action. You'll most likely see a later S model, with its dramatic, optional rear wing designed to stop the car taking off at high speeds – Countachs can reach almost 180mph.

I-SPY points: 40

Date:

MORRIS MARINA
1971-1980

The Marina gained a reputation for mediocre driving characteristics because of its old-fashioned suspension system. But that didn't stop it becoming a million-seller for it was, at heart, a reliable car. Engines ranged from 1.3- to 1.8-litre, and there was a choice of two-door coupé, four-door saloon and five-door estate.

I-SPY points: 15

Date: _____

ASTON MARTIN V8
1972-1990

First seen as the DBS V8 in 1969, this fast, prestigious and expensive car became simply the V8 three years later with a distinctive re-style at the front. The entire car is handbuilt, even down to the 5.3-litre V8 engine. It can do 145mph, even more in highly-tuned Vantage form, and there's also a luxurious convertible edition, called the Volante.

I-SPY points: 30

Date: _____

42

FIAT X1/9 *1972-1989*

This compact two-seater sports car has a lift-out roof panel to delight fresh air freaks. The engine is mid-mounted. It's cramped inside for tall drivers, but ride quality, road-holding and handling are exceptional. The first 1.3-litre version was a 100mph car, while the later 1.5 (identifiable by bigger bumpers) managed 111mph.

I-SPY points: 20

Date: _____

RENAULT 5 MK 1
1972-1984

What's particularly special about this little car? Well, it was the very first 'supermini', a compact city car with a hatchback and folding rear seats. It set the template for many later rivals. These early, straight-lined 5s have distinctive plastic bumpers, but seeing one is unusual: the car suffered rust problems, so most are no longer on the road.

I-SPY points: 20

Date: _____

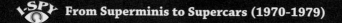

AUSTIN ALLEGRO
1973-1983

This small family car, built as a saloon and an estate, was launched by British Leyland to replace its long-running 1100/1300 series. Buyers were none too keen on the podgy new styling or the strange 'square' steering wheel. But those surviving examples are much-loved today.

I-SPY points: 20

Date: _____

CATERHAM SEVEN
1973-today

The origins of this slender two–seater go all the way back to the Lotus Seven of 1957; Caterham Cars have built it since 1973. Often compared to a four-wheeled motorbike, occupants are strapped in close to the ground, and the Caterham chassis allows fantastic, racing car-style responses even with less powerful engines.

I-SPY points: 25

Date: _____

RELIANT ROBIN
1973-1982

This original Robin is the most successful three-wheeled car ever sold in Britain. To keep weight down – so the Robin could legally qualify as a tricycle, and so be driven on a motorbike license – the two-door body is plastic, and the tiny four-cylinder engine is made of aluminium. It's an extremely cheap car to run.

I-SPY points: 20

Date: _____

VOLVO 240 ESTATE
1974-1993

Volvo estates like this were always popular with people such as antique dealers and others, like farmers, who needed to tow trailers. Not only is the square rear compartment spacious for cargo, but the 240 is extraordinarily sturdy, with plenty of safety features; these cars seem to go on forever.

I-SPY points: 10

Date: _____

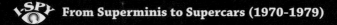
FERRARI 308 GTS
1975-1981

This was the car that took the place of the 246 Dino in Ferrari's range and, although it uses some of the same components beneath those breathtaking lines, the engine is a 3.0-litre V8. The roof panel can be removed and the air intakes along the side are highly distinctive.

I-SPY points: 30

Date: _____

JAGUAR XJ-S
1975-1996

The XJ-S divided opinion. Some were not partial to its styling, which included metal 'buttresses' at the back, but most people admired the fabulously silken 150mph performance from its V12 engine, and its sumptuous cabin. There were other engine options and two kinds of convertible – one with a roll-over bar and its replacement without.

I-SPY points: 10

Date: _____

FORD FIESTA MKI
1976-1983

Ford's entry in the booming 'supermini' class of the 1970s was an instant hit with drivers all over Europe, who liked its predictable, front-wheel drive driving style and neat design. You might see one of the 1981-84 XR2 versions, a 1.6-litre sports model with unique 'pepper pot'-style alloy wheels.

I-SPY points: 20

Date: _____

VW GOLF GTI MK1
1976-1983

Volkswagen has built 6.9m MkI Golfs, and indeed it's still manufactured in South Africa as a cheap family car. This superb, front-wheel drive hatchback provided the basis for the GTi, which boasts a fuel-injected 1.6-litre (later 1.8-litre, too) engine, stiffened suspension and wide wheels; sporty drivers loved it and it was the iconic hot-hatch of the day.

I-SPY points: 20

Date: _____

PORSCHE 928
1977-1995

By putting the engine – a V8 – in the front of a high-performance sports car, Porsche broke all its own traditions. Starting at 4.5-litre, it eventually grew into a 5.0-litre, four-seater supercar, capable of almost 170mph. It remains the only sports car ever to win the European Car Of The Year award.

I-SPY points: 30

Date: _____

SAAB 900
1978-1993

This was a range of cars with a specifically Swedish character that gained, over its long life, an enviable reputation for safety and comfort. They all share derivatives of the same 2.0-litre engine which, when fitted with a turbocharger, can propel a 900 to over 130mph. Look out for the attractive Saab 900 convertible, too.

I-SPY points: 10

Date: _____

AUDI QUATTRO
1980-1991

The four-wheel drive Quattro made a sensational debut in 1980, and led to a range of models; hence 'Quattro' came to be used for Audi's whole 4x4 family. It transformed the idea of what made a successful rally car. Although a large and heavy car, the turbocharged 2.1-litre engine propels it to 132mph. The Quattro proved hugely successful in rallying.

I-SPY points: 25

Date: _____

FIAT PANDA MKI
1980-2003

This tiny four-seater resembles a box on wheels – even the windscreen and side glass are completely flat! It was intended for everyday economy and practicality. The 1.0-litre engine was light on fuel, but four-wheel drive was offered.

I-SPY points: 15

Date: _____

49

LOTUS ESPRIT TURBO *1980-1987*

This is the ultra high-performance version of a radical, mid-engined two-seater first introduced in 1976. All of Lotus's handling and roadholding virtues are evident, and the 210bhp of energy from the turbocharged 2.2-litre engine makes this a 150mph machine. Side skirts and spoilers keep it anchored to the tarmac.

I-SPY points: 30

Date: _____

ROLLS-ROYCE SILVER SPIRIT *1980-1989*

Rolls-Royce offered its traditional dignity and soothing comfort with the Silver Spirit (a similar model with more rear passenger space, the Silver Spur, could be ordered with a glass division between chauffeur and passengers). The 6.7-litre V8 gave a maximum speed of 120mph – but, of course, terrible fuel economy!

I-SPY points: 15

Date: _____

DELOREAN DMC-12 *1981-1982*

You won't see many of these gullwing-door coupés here because, despite being manufactured in Northern Ireland, most were exported to the USA. The bodywork is of unpainted stainless steel panels, and the rear-mounted engine is a 2.8-litre Renault V6. It was a notorious sales flop but did star in the *Back To The Future* movie series.

I-SPY points: 45

Date: _____

MERCEDES-BENZ 500SEC *1981-1986*

Mercedes-Benz's costly, top of the range coupé for the early 1980s was almost in the Rolls-Royce class for effortless refinement; its 5.0-litre V8 engine affords it a top speed of 142mph, although a less thirsty 3.0-litre engine could be chosen instead. All the side windows can be lowered to give a cool 'pillar-less' look for cruising.

I-SPY points: 20

Date: _____

TRIUMPH ACCLAIM *1981-1984*

This neat saloon was a Honda Ballade built under license by British Leyland, in its quest to breathe new life into the British car industry; as such, it's the first Japanese car to have been built in Europe. Light controls and a quiet engine made it well-liked.

I-SPY points: 30

Date: _____

FORD SIERRA
1982-1992

After the ultra-conventional Cortina, its replacement made a huge impact with its 'jellymould' profile and its ergonomically designed interior. Today, it doesn't look at all strange! Britain bought millions of Sierras, but few survive unless they are the high-performance Cosworth versions, with spectacular aerofoil spoilers at the back.

I-SPY points: 15

Date: _____

LADA RIVA
1982-today

Still being manufactured in Russia today, the rugged Riva (as saloon or estate) can actually trace its roots back to the Fiat 124 of 1966. Designed primarily for the punishing road conditions found in its homeland, engines ranged from 1.2- to 1.6-litre, and they were sold at bargain prices.

I-SPY points: 15

Date:

TOYOTA MR-2 MKI
1984-1989

The 'M' stands for mid-engined, the 'R' for recreational, and the 2 for two-seater. Toyota provided fine-handling fun with this sports car. The engine is a 1.6-litre that sucks in cooling air through vents situated behind the doors. You may see one with a 'T-bar' open roof, an option from 1988.

I-SPY points: 25

Date:

FERRARI F40
1987-1992

Introduced to mark Ferrari's 40th year of building exotic sports cars, this was also – for a brief period – the world's fastest production car, with a claimed 201mph maximum.

Its turbocharged 3-litre V8 was behind the two-seat cockpit. No mistaking that gigantic rear aerofoil. But it's a rare sight on the road.

I-SPY points: 45

Date:

VAUXHALL LOTUS CARLTON *1988-1992*

The basic Carlton was a straightforward executive saloon, but once sports car specialist Lotus had been let loose on it, it had a 3.6-litre twin-turbo engine, a massive 377bhp on tap, and potential to reach 180mph; there's a six-speed gearbox, too. The wide wheels, side skirts and substantial spoilers identify it. A wool in sheep's clothing!

I-SPY points: 40

Date:

MAZDA MX-5 MK I *1989-1998*

Pretty small sports cars like this used to be a British speciality, but Mazda took over from where MG and Triumph left off with this neat little roadster. The 1.6- or 1.8-litre engines feed power to the rear wheels in time-honoured sports car fashion. Pop-up headlights keep the front looking sleek – during the day, anyway!

I-SPY points: 10

Date:

VAUXHALL CALIBRA *1989-1997*

Beneath the wind-cheating styling, the Calibra shared its mechanical parts with the humble Vauxhall Cavalier. Despite the low roofline, the Calibra's still a two-door full four-seater, with a hatchback leading on to a roomy luggage compartment. Besides the standard 2.0-litre engine, there's a turbo edition, plus a 2.5-litre V6.

I-SPY points: 10

Date:

HONDA NSX
1990-2006

With supercar lines suggesting it hails from Italy rather than Japan, the NSX is far removed from the Civic, Accord and CR-V for which Honda is known. Although looks, engineering and performance – from a mid-mounted 3.0- or 3.2-litre V6 – were definitely in Ferrari territory, the NSX was docile and easy enough to drive to the local supermarket.

I-SPY points: 30

Date:

TVR GRIFFITH
1991-2002

The last TVR was made in 2005 but, until then, these Blackpool-built sports cars had been among the most exciting and powerful British cars on sale. The Griffith is also one of the most best-looking. Its V8 engine range culminates in a 5.0-litre, giving a 167mph top speed. Note the rear lights...taken from a Vauxhall Cavalier.

I-SPY points: 25

Date:

MCLAREN F1
1992-1998

The most striking
visual feature of this
compact supercar is
its central driving
position, like a
Formula 1 car; features
of this compact
supercar
are its up-and over
doors. A vary rare
sight on any road!

I-SPY points: 50

Date: _____

MGF *1995-2002*

A popular British two-seater
sports car, this was the first MG
with its engine mounted behind
the driver and passenger. There
are 1.6- and 1.8-litre versions.
From 2002, it was restyled
to become the MG TF, with
prominent side skirts, and this
car is still in limited production at
a Birmingham factory.

I-SPY points: 10

Date: _____

LOTUS ELISE
MK I *1995-2001*

Norfolk-based sports car legend Lotus turned the corner with the Elise. It's a small and nimble sports car with a 1.6-litre engine positioned behind the driver. Enthusiasts love its racing-car style handling, which is helped by sophisticated aluminium/glassfibre construction.

I-SPY points: 15

Date: _____

FORD PUMA
1997-2001

Like the Fiesta it's based on, the Puma is front-engined and front-wheel drive, but its unique body design is a compact, low-roofed coupé, with seating for four. There were mild 1.4- and 1.6-litre four-cylinder engines, and a special 1.7-litre for sparkling acceleration. It was BBC *Top Gear's* favourite car of 1997.

I-SPY points: 10

Date: _____

AUDI TT MK I
1998-2006

The curvaceous contours of these cars was inspired by 1930s product and racing car design, although the TT shares parts with many other Volkswagen Group-made cars. There is a wide choice: coupe or convertible, two- or four-wheel drive, and 1.8-litre turbo or 3.2-litre non-turbo engine.

I-SPY points: 10

Date: _____

SUBARU IMPREZA TURBO MKI
1993-2004

The four-wheel drive Impreza Turbo proved a phenomenal rally car, bagging the World Rally Championship for Subaru three times between 1995-97. In 1995, too, the car made driver Colin McRae Britain's first World Rally champion. Road car versions offered up to 300bhp, 0-62mph in 4.6sec and 155mph top speed.

I-SPY points: 15

Date: _____

MERCEDES-BENZ SLK MKI *1996-2004*

This two-seater sports car caused excitement by having a folding metal top instead of a canvas hood. The roof could be lowered in one operation simply by pressing a button. The first model had a 2.3-litre four-cylinder, supercharged engine; in this form, the car can reach 140mph. Later there were several engine choices available.

I-SPY points: 10

Date:

SMART FORTWO MKI *1998-2008*

Everyone knows it as "the Smart car" but you'll notice early ones are badged 'MCC Smart City-Coupé' (MCC stands for Micro Compact Car). The tiny city runabout has a 0.7-litre three-cylinder motor at the back, tucked away under the two seats. The design allows Smarts to be customized by their owners, so you'll rarely see two alike.

I-SPY points: 10

Date:

BMW Z8 *2000-2003*

A rare and beautiful sports
car from BMW, with a front-
mounted, 4.9-litre V8 engine
driving the rear wheels and a
top speed electronically limited
to 155mph. The two-seater
cockpit features wonderful
leather-and-chrome trim. Pierce
Brosnan, as *James Bond*, drove
one in the 1999 film *The World Is
Not Enough*.

I-SPY points: 35

Date: _____

MORGAN AERO 8
2000-today

It has the vague outline
of a vintage car, and its
bodywork is handbuilt
over a wooden framework.
But the amazing Aero 8
offers an exciting driving
experience from the
4.4-litre V8 engine under
its long, long bonnet. An
unusual Morgan feature is the
triple windscreen wipers.

I-SPY points: 35

Date: _____

BENTLEY STATE LIMOUSINE
2002

This is a car you'll only see on royal occasions because it was designed and built specially for Her Majesty Queen Elizabeth as she goes about Britain on ceremonial duties. Presented during her golden jubilee, the rear compartment affords a good view of the monarch, and allows a dignified entrance and exit.

I-SPY points: 40

Date: _____

BUGATTI VEYRON
2005-today

The result of a no-compromise effort to revive the Bugatti name, the Veyron is the world's fastest production car, with a 253mph maximum speed. An incredible 8 litre 16 cylinder W16 engine can be seen through a glass engine cover at the back. It has four-wheel drive, seven gears, 10 radiators and 1001 brake horsepower.

I-SPY points: 50

Date: _____

Index

AC/Shelby Cobra 27
Alfa Romeo Spider 34
Amphicar 24
Aston Martin DB5 29
Aston Martin V8 42
Audi Quattro 49
Audi TT Mk I 59
Austin 10 8
Austin Allegro 44
Austin FX4 taxi 20
Austin Maxi 37
Austin Seven 6
Austin-Healey 3000 22
Austin-Healey Sprite
  Mk I 21
Bentley 3-litre 6
Bentley R-type
  Continental 17
Bentley State
  Limousine 62
BMW Isetta 18
BMW Z8 61
Bond Bug 39
Bristol 400 12
Bugatti Veyron 62
Caterham Seven 44
Citroen 'Traction
  Avant' 9
Citroën 2CV 12
Citroën DS19 18
Citroën Type C 5
Datsun 240Z 39
De-Dion Bouton 3
Delorean DMC-12 51
Ferrari 308 GTS 46
Ferrari 365 GTB/4 35
Ferrari Dino 246
  GT 37
Ferrari F40 54
Fiat 500 7
Fiat Panda Mk I 49
Fiat X1/9 43
Ford Anglia 105E 22

Ford Capri Mk1 38
Ford Consul Mk I 16
Ford Cortina Mk III 40
Ford Fiesta MkI 47
Ford Model T 4
Ford Model Y 8hp 8
Ford Mustang I 30
Ford Puma 58
Ford Sierra 52
Hillman Imp 28
Honda NSX 56
Jaguar E-type 24
Jaguar Mk II 23
Jaguar Mk X 25
Jaguar XJ-S 46
Jaguar XK120 13
Jensen Interceptor 33
Jowett Javelin 14
Lada Riva 53
Lamborghini
  Countach 41
Lancia Aprilia 10
Lancia Fulvia
  Coupé 30
Land Rover Series 1 13
Lotus Elan 27
Lotus Elise Mk I 58
Lotus Esprit Turbo 50
Lotus Europa 33
Mazda MX-5 Mk I 55
McLaren F1 57
Mercedes-Benz
  280SL 34
Mercedes-Benz
  500SEC 51
Mercedes-Benz SLK
  Mk I 60
MG Midget 25
MG TA Midget 9
MG TD 15
MGB GT 31
MGF 57
Mini Cooper 26

Morgan Aero 8 61
Morgan Plus 8 36
Morris Cowley 5
Morris Marina 42
Morris Minor 7
Morris Minor 14
NSU Ro80 14
Porsche 356 16
Porsche 911 28
Porsche 928 48
Range Rover 40
Reliant Robin 45
Reliant Scimitar
  GTE 38
Renault 16 31
Renault 5 Mk 1 43
Renault Dauphine 19
Rolls-Royce Silver
  Spirit 50
Rolls-Royce 20/25 7
Rolls-Royce 40/50hp 3
Rolls-Royce Silver
  Shadow 32
Rover P6 29
Saab 900 48
SAAB 96 32

Smart Fortwo Mk I 60
SS 100 Jaguar 10
Subaru Impreza
  Turbo Mk I 59
Toyota MR-2 MkI 53
Triumph Acclaim 52
Triumph Herald 23
Triumph Renown 15
Triumph Stag 41
Triumph TR2 17
TVR Griffith 56
Vauxhall Calibra 55
Vauxhall Cresta PA 21
Vauxhall Lotus
  Carlton 54
Vauxhall Prince
  Henry 4
Volkswagen Beetle 11
Volkswagen
  Karmann-Ghia 19
Volkswagen
  Transporter Kombi 36
Volvo 240 estate 45
Volvo P1800 26
VW Golf GTi Mk1 47
Willys Jeep MB 11

First published by Michelin Maps and Guides 2009 ©
Michelin, Proprietaires-Editeurs 2009. Michelin and the
Michelin Man are registered Trademarks of Michelin.
Created and produced by Horizons Publishing Limited.
All rights reserved. No part of this publication may be
reproduced, copied or transmitted in any form without
the prior consent of the publisher.
Print services by FingerPrint International Book
production – fingerprint@pandora.be
The publisher gratefully acknowledges the contribution
of the I-Spy team: Camilla Lovell and Sheila Watts in
the production of this title.
The publisher gratefully acknowledges the contribution
of Giles Chapman, who compiled the contents and
wrote the text.
Many of the photographs used in this book are © Neill
Bruce. The publisher also gratefully acknowledges his
assistance in sourcing further images from the following
manufacturers: Aston Martin, Audi, BMW, Bristol,
Bugatti, Citroën, Fiat, Ford, Jaguar, Lada, Lancia, Lotus,
Mazda, Mercedes-Benz, Renault, Saab, Smart, Toyota,
Vauxhall, Volkswagen and Volvo.
Additional photographs were supplied by the Giles
Chapman Library.

HOW TO GET YOUR I-SPY CERTIFICATE AND BADGE

Every time you score 1000 points or more in an I-Spy book, you can apply for a certificate

Here's what to do, step by step:

Certificate

- Ask an adult to check your score
- Ask his or her permission to apply for a certificate
- Apply online to www.ispymichelin.com
- Enter your name and address and the completed title
- We will send you back via e mail your certificate for the title

Badge

- Each I-Spy title has a cut out (page corner) token at the back of the book
- Collect five tokens from different I-Spy titles
- Put Second Class Stamps on two strong envelopes
- Write your own address on one envelope and put a £1 coin inside it (for protection). Fold, but do not seal the envelope, and place it inside the second envelope
- Write the following address on the second envelope, seal it carefully and post to:

I-Spy Books
Michelin Maps and Guides
Hannay House
39 Clarendon Road
Watford
WD17 1JA